I0866707

TABLE OF CONTENTS

WARM-UP TALK

Talk about Awkward

Ever had an awkward conversation? Maybe something like this?

Talking can be tricky sometimes. We've all had awkward conversations. Awkwardness happens when we aren't really sure what to say. It makes us uncomfortable, but it can also make us laugh. So, let's get started with some fun awkwardness. Fill in the speech bubbles and create your own awkward conversation.

PRAYING WITH JESUS

THE LORD'S PRAYER FOR KIDS

THE FOUNDRY
KIDS

The Foundry Publishing
PO Box 419527, Kansas City, MO 64141
thefoundrypublishing.com

ISBN 978-0-8341-3979-4
Printed in the United States of America

Cover & Interior Design: J.R. Caines
Writer: Jeremy Bond
Editors: Kimberly A. Crenshaw & Kyle Tyler

10 9 8 7 6 5 4 3 2 1

Talk about Talking

Now that the awkwardness is out of the way, let's talk about prayer. Prayer is spending time *with* God, which includes talking *to* God. That's why prayer feels awkward sometimes. It can feel awkward because *talking* can feel awkward.

Plus, we can't see God. So we're talking with someone we can't see. That feels a little different too. We don't want to say something weird. And we for sure don't want to say something *super* weird.

Here's the good news. God understands. Jesus understands. Jesus wants to help us feel comfortable talking to God. He wants to help us pray. In fact, Jesus gave us sort of a sample prayer to help us out. We call it the Lord's Prayer. Maybe you've heard of it. Maybe you haven't. Either way, this book is going to help you explore prayer by looking at the prayer Jesus taught, the Lord's Prayer.

You might be thinking, "Hey, I'm great at this praying stuff. My prayers are better than cat videos and tacos." Well, great! Guess what? The Lord's Prayer is still for you. Everyone can learn something new from the Lord's Prayer. How does the Lord's Prayer help us out? How can it make prayer less awkward? We'll get to that.

First, take a few minutes and think about prayer. Write down how you feel about prayer in the space below. What's hard about it? What's easy? What do you love about it? How does it make you nervous? Or, draw a picture of how you feel when you pray. In other words, write down anything that comes to mind when you think about praying.

WARNING

You Won't Get Better

This book won't make you better at praying. Why not? God loves *all* of our prayers. He loves it when we want to spend time with Him. Prayers can't be better or worse just because of the words we choose. He won't ignore your prayer if you sound awkward, open your eyes, or sneeze in the middle of it.

Don't think of this book as a way to get *better* at praying. Instead, think of it as a way to understand prayer, discover something new about prayer, and enjoy prayer. Think of it as a way to explore your relationship with Jesus by exploring prayer. And, of course, think of it as a way to feel less awkward when you pray.

Wake Up. Warm Up.

Before we explore the Lord's Prayer, there's something we should understand first. Jesus prayed. He didn't just talk about prayer. He actually prayed. Check it out.

***It was very early in the morning and still dark. Jesus got up and left the house. He went to a place where he could be alone. There he prayed. Simon and his friends went to look for Jesus. When they found him, they called out, "Everyone is looking for you!"* Mark 1:35-37 (NIrV)**

Have you ever woken up so early that it was still dark outside? Jesus must have been a morning person. At least, He was a morning person on this day. Don't worry. This doesn't mean you have to wake up super early when it's not even a school day. Look at the passage again. Then, do some exploring.

Circle the sentence in the passage that shows why you think Jesus got up so early in the morning.

Draw a box around the words that show where He went after He woke up.

Underline the name of the person who finally found Him.

Jesus just wanted to be alone to pray. He wanted to be alone with God. We don't know how long Jesus prayed, but it probably wasn't too long before Simon tapped Him on the shoulder. Verse 37 shows us that Jesus was a popular guy that morning. "Everyone is looking for you!" they said.

This isn't the only time we read about Jesus praying. When you have some quiet time of your own, check out these three stories and see what you can find.

> ***CHALLENGE:*** Keep reading after verse 37 to see what Jesus did after He prayed. Read as much as you want. See if you find anything that might give us a clue as to what He was praying about that morning. We can't know for sure, but what do you think?

Luke 3:21-22 shows the heavens opened up when Jesus prayed. God spoke out loud too. That's pretty awesome.

Matthew 14:22-24 shows Jesus didn't always wake up super early to pray. He also stayed up super late. As a bonus, this kicks off a story where people think they saw a ghost. That's pretty awesome too.

Luke 9:28-29 starts with Jesus praying up on a mountain with His friends and disciples, Peter, John, and James. That sounds pretty normal, but the story soon takes a wild turn and gets really awesome, really fast.

The Lord's Prayer. Let's Do This.

We aren't the only ones who have questions about prayer. Jesus's disciples even had questions. Maybe they felt awkward when they talked to God. Maybe they saw Jesus praying by himself and they got curious. Whatever the reason, they wanted Jesus to show them how to pray. Jesus did just that with the Lord's Prayer.

Let's explore the Lord's Prayer found in **Matthew 6:9-13** (NIV). It's part of a long sermon that Jesus preached called the Sermon on the Mount. You ready for this? Here's the prayer:

Our Father in heaven,
hallowed be your name,
your kingdom come,
your will be done,
on earth as it is in heaven.
Give us today our daily bread.
And forgive us our debts,
as we also have forgiven our debtors.
And lead us not into temptation,
but deliver us from the evil one,
for yours is the kingdom and the power
and the glory forever.

Amen.

That's the Lord's Prayer. Maybe you've heard it before. Maybe you even have it memorized. But knowing all the words and knowing what it all means are different. So, here's what's going to happen. We're going to divide this prayer into six parts and look at each part on its own. Looking at smaller chunks makes it easier to understand what Jesus is trying to teach us.

Also, as we look at the Lord's Prayer, we'll use five questions to guide us as we go. We ask ourselves these questions to help us understand and explore any Scripture, including the Lord's Prayer. Most of the time, you won't actually see these questions in print, but if you watch closely, you'll discover answers to these questions as you go. The questions are called ***The 5 What's***.

1. ***What's that word?*** It's hard to understand a passage if we don't know what the words mean. Like that word *hallowed*. Yeah, what does that mean? We'll find out.

2. ***What's happening in the passage?*** This is where we figure out the basics of what's going on. For example, you already know the Lord's Prayer is part of a sermon. So, one thing that's happening is that Jesus is preaching. See, you're getting the hang of this already.

3. ***What's happening in the Bible?*** This is where we see how other parts of the Bible can help us understand the Lord's Prayer. We've already started on this one too. Remember back a few pages when we looked at a few Bible stories of Jesus praying?

4. ***What's this say about God?*** Anytime we read Scripture, we're getting to know God better. The Bible is the beginning of God's big gigantic story of awesomeness. What can we find in the Lord's Prayer to help us understand God's awesomeness better?

5. ***What's this say about us?*** Let's see what the Lord's Prayer can show us about ourselves. What can we discover about why we pray or how we pray? Goodbye, awkwardness!

FROM "OUR FATHER" TO "YOUR NAME"

Our Father in heaven, hallowed be your name.

First, let's look at a few words from this part of the prayer.

Our: Us. Everybody. Community. God is there for all of us. We are all part of His family. We belong together. Even if you're in your room, hiding behind the clothes in your closet, wearing a football helmet, and closing your eyes, you aren't praying alone. Millions of Christians around the world pray every day.

Father: Okay, you know what a father is, but Jesus adds a twist. He says, "Father in heaven," so He's giving us a specific way to think about God. God created us. He listens. He loves us no matter what. We're part of His family. Fathers on earth aren't perfect, but our Father in heaven sure is. God is like the perfect parent.

Hallowed: Holy or worthy of our worship, respect, amazement, and love. God's name is hallowed because God is perfect, powerful, and full of love.

When we pray, let's remember that God *wants* to talk to us. We aren't bugging Him when we pray. Yes, He's holy and powerful. Even His name is hallowed. We pray with respect and praise and worship. But Jesus says that God is also like a perfect parent. You are part of His family. He *wants* to hear from you. He's our Creator, and He *loves* it when we talk to Him, listen to Him, and spend time with Him.

Spend some quiet time with God thinking about this part of the prayer. Here are a few options to inspire your time with God:

A. Draw a picture of yourself as part of God's family.

B. Write as many words you can think of that describe God.

C. Write about something important you see in this part of the Lord's Prayer.

YOUR KINGDOM COME

Your kingdom come, your will be done, on earth as it is in heaven.

Kingdom: God's actions to deliver people from the power of sin, love them like crazy, and bring peace to all things. Think of kingdom as an action word or a place where God is active. It's God's actions in people to make things right in the world. He's our Creator. God has the love, power, and authority to be our King.

God is acting in the world right now. He's making it better each day, but there's much more to come. That's why sometimes God's kingdom sounds like it's way off in the future, and sometimes it sounds like it's right here and right now. It's both. God's kingdom will be totally perfect when He's finished.

What does Jesus say about the kingdom in this prayer? Are we *saying* something or *asking* for something? Yes. Both. Jesus says that God's kingdom *will* come. It's going to happen, but it's also happening already. In fact, the kingdom was standing right there teaching people how to pray. How's that?

Kingdom is sometimes called the "kingdom of God" or the "kingdom of heaven." Matthew used "kingdom of heaven" as a respectful way to avoid saying God's name, so both phrases can be used for kingdom.

Remember: Think of kingdom as an *action* word. What's the biggest action God has taken in the world since He created it? He sent Jesus! Jesus is the kingdom, and He was standing right there in front of everyone, teaching them to pray.

When we pray like this, we praise God for the actions He's taking in the world, including sending Jesus himself. We thank Him for saving people from the power of sin, for loving everyone like crazy, and for bringing peace to the world. We praise Him because it's happening, and then we look forward to what else He's going to do. Not just in *other* people, but in *us*.

We also tell God that we *want* His kingdom to come, and we want to be part of it. It's like we're saying, "God, I want my actions to be like your actions. I want my love to be like your love."

That's a big statement. Huge. Not only are we telling God we want things on earth to be just the way He wants them, we're also saying we want God to act through our own lives to make it happen. We're saying that we are willing to be part of God's kingdom, God's loving actions. We're ready to live in His loving holiness.

Spend some quiet time with God thinking about this part of the prayer. Here are a few options to inspire your time with God:

A. Draw a picture of part of God's kingdom, a picture of God taking action in our world.

B. Write as many words you can think of to describe God's kingdom.

C. Write about something important you've discovered in this part of the Lord's Prayer.

TIME OUT

Let's take a short break. It won't take too long, and it will help us understand prayer. Promise. Let's jump over to Matthew 19 and see what happened a few chapters *after* Jesus taught the Lord's Prayer.

Jesus and His disciples are hanging out near the Jordan River answering questions. In the middle of this teaching time, somebody tried to bring some kids up to Jesus. Here's what happened.

Some people brought little children to Jesus. They wanted him to place his hands on the children and pray for them. But the disciples told them not to do it. Jesus said, "Let the little children come to me. Don't keep them away. The kingdom of heaven belongs to people like them." Jesus placed his hands on them to bless them. Then he went on from there. **Matthew 19:13-15 (NIrV)**

This part of God's story is great for lots of reasons. Let's focus on two of them. First, it shows Jesus living what He described in the first line of the Lord's Prayer. Remember, God wants us to know He's like a parent who loves spending time with us. That's what happens here.

Kids are brought to Jesus so Jesus can bless them and pray for them, but the disciples must be stressed out or something. How do they react? They tell the group with the kids to leave Jesus alone. Rude. But Jesus isn't having it. He wants to bless those kids, so He calls them over and does just that. But that's not all He does. Now, let's talk about the second great thing.

Jesus says the kingdom of heaven belongs to anyone like these kids. In other words, anyone who wants to spend time with God is welcome. In Bible times, it was easy to think about kids as not super important. That's a major bummer. Jesus sure didn't think that way. Not only did He teach everyone that kids were part of God's kingdom and family, but anyone who was like these kids was part of it too.

You don't have to be someone important to be important to God. God's kingdom is for everyone. God wants to spend time with you. You don't have to be super important or super old or super good at talking. You just have to be you.

DAILY BREAD

Give us today our daily bread.

God provides. It's that simple. Sometimes He does it with a miracle that surprises everyone. Sometimes He does it in ways we barely notice. The important part is this: *Jesus cares about our daily needs. He's a friend.*

Paul understood this. He encouraged the people at his church to go to God at any time for any need. Here's part of his letter:

Don't worry about anything. No matter what happens, tell God about everything. Ask and pray, and give thanks to him. Then God's peace will watch over your hearts and your minds. He will do this because you belong to Christ Jesus. God's peace can never be completely understood. **Philippians 4:6-7 (NIrV)**

That's pretty great guidance. Instead of worrying, we can tell God about *everything* we need, even energy to finish homework. Whatever it is, we can ask and He'll watch over us. Paul is speaking from experience. He knows what it's like to be worried. He knows what it's like to be hungry. A few sentences later, he says this:

I know what it's like not to have what I need. I also know what it's like to have more than I need. I have learned the secret of being content no matter what happens. I am content whether I am well fed or hungry. I am content whether I have more than enough or not enough. I can do all this by the power of Christ. He gives me strength. **Philippians 4:12-13 (NIrV)**

Does anything stand out to you in that passage? Paul said God's strength allowed him to be content with whatever he had or didn't have. Being content doesn't mean he *liked* being

without things. It didn't even mean he stopped looking for help. It just meant he was at peace with whatever he had or didn't have.

There's one little word in this part of the Lord's Prayer that's easy to miss. It starts with the letter "d." See it?

The word is *daily*. Daily bread. After we see what Jesus said a few minutes later in His sermon, it's easy to see why He used the word *daily*.

Don't store up treasures here on earth, where moths eat them and rust destroys them, and where thieves break in and steal. Store your treasures in heaven, where moths and rust cannot destroy, and thieves do not break in and steal. Wherever your treasure is, there the desires of your heart will also be. **Matthew 6:19-21 (NLT)**

Jesus warns us about the dangers of obsessing about getting more and more and more of everything. If all we want is *more*, then all we'll get is disappointment. That's why Jesus said *daily* bread. Let's trust Him each day. Love Him each day. Walk with Him each day.

One more thing. Remember how the first line of the Lord's Prayer says *Our* Father? The word *our* appears here too. When we pray, we aren't just praying for ourselves. We're praying for others too. We're praying for the daily needs of those around us. We want their needs met just as much as ours.

Sometimes, *we* can be the way God answers a prayer for someone else. Think about this. If you provide a meal for another family, *you* become an answer to that family's prayer. When you help someone, you become part of God's answer to that person's prayer. That's pretty great.

Spend some quiet time with God thinking about this part of the prayer. Here are a few options to inspire your time with God:

A. Draw a picture of how God provides for you each day.

B. Write as many ways that you can think of to help provide for the people around you.

C. Write about something important you see in this part of the Lord's Prayer.

FORGIVE US. WE FORGIVE.

And forgive us our debts, as we also have forgiven our debtors.

Debt and Debtors: You might also see *trespasses* or *sin* used instead of *debt*. These are all words for times we disobey God or make selfish choices that hurt others. They also describe people or actions that hurt us.

Okay, this is when the prayer starts to get hard. It's honesty time. Now is the time Jesus wants us to think about anything that needs to be forgiven. Choices we've made. Choices others have made. It's time to take them to Jesus.

Let's start with us. Have our words or actions hurt someone? Have we asked that person for forgiveness? What have we done that needs forgiving? Those are hard questions to answer truthfully. That's the bad news. The good news is Jesus forgives. He's our Savior, King, and Friend.

He *forgives* us because He's our Savior. He has *power* over sin because He's our King. He *loves* to forgive us because He's our Friend. Once we bring our debts, trespasses, sins, or bad choices to Jesus, we can leave them there.

This part of the prayer isn't there to make us feel bad about ourselves. Nope. It's there for the opposite reason. It's there to free us, encourage us, and remind us of God's love for us. Receiving forgiveness gives us confidence and hope.

That confidence and hope will help with the next part. That's when we forgive those who have made choices that have hurt us. Because God loves and forgives us, we have the strength to forgive others. Of course, that doesn't make it easy.

If you forgive someone, that doesn't mean you think what they did was okay. It also doesn't mean you'll instantly forget it ever happened. And, just as important, it doesn't give them permission to do it again.

If someone hurts you, it doesn't need to stay a secret. Tell someone you trust about it, and let that person help you through it. In really tough times, we need trusted and loving people to help us out so we can feel safe again.

Here's what forgiveness *is*. Forgiveness means letting go of anger. We give God our anger so it stops bouncing around in our heads and causing us more problems. That's not easy. Actually, sometimes it's really hard.

That's why we let God's love fill us up. That's why we go to God first before we try to forgive. Feel the perfect love God has for you. He created you. *You did not deserve to be hurt. God's not okay with it either. Let His love fill you up so you can love yourself.* Have confidence because you are God's creation. You're part of God's family. That's where forgiveness begins.

Spend some quiet time with God thinking about this part of the prayer. Here are a few options to inspire your time with God:

A. Draw a picture of how it feels to be forgiven or how it feels to forgive.

B. Write as many words you can think of to describe forgiveness.

C. Write about something you thought about as you explored this part of the Lord's Prayer.

LEAD US NOT

And lead us not into temptation, but deliver us from the evil one.

Peirasmos: Wait. What? This word isn't in the Lord's Prayer. Also, what is this word? Actually, it *is* in the Lord's Prayer. *Peirasmos* is a Greek word that was used when the book of Matthew was originally written. It has a couple of meanings.

First, it means *temptation*, a desire to do something wrong. *Peirasmos* also means *testing*. Testing is when we go through something hard that helps us grow in faith. The goal of temptation is to get us to do wrong. The goal of testing is to make us stronger in our faith.

Let's get one thing straight. *God does not tempt us*. At first, we might read this part of the prayer and think God tempts us, but that's not what's happening. James 1:13 makes this clear:

And remember, when you are being tempted, do not say, "God is tempting me." God is never tempted to do wrong, and he never tempts anyone else. **James 1:13 (NLT)**

That's why understanding the original word *peirasmos* is super helpful. When we understand *peirasmos*, then we can see more clearly how Jesus is telling us to pray.

When we pray, we can ask for strength to get us through hard times of *testing*. We want those struggles to grow our faith and make our lives with Jesus stronger. We don't want those struggles to lead to *temptation* to give up, do wrong, or turn away from God. Remember, *temptation* tries to make us weaker. *Testing* tries to make us stronger.

We can make it through tough times when we rely on God.

He's the one who gives us power to stomp out evil temptations that come our way. God is taking action in the world. He makes us stronger through tough times.

Last thing. Remember, this prayer says *our* and *us* and *we*. We were created to have friendships with other people who love Jesus and help us through temptation. Let other Christians encourage you, give you advice, or help you out. Together, we can do this!

Spend some quiet time with God thinking about this part of the prayer. Here are a few options to inspire your time with God:

A. Draw a picture of God having power over evil.

B. Write as many words you can think of that will give you encouragement during tough times.

C. Write about something important you discovered in this part of the Lord's Prayer.

AMEN

For yours is the kingdom and the power and the glory forever. Amen.

You've probably heard or seen this part of the prayer, but it's nowhere to be found in the Bible. What gives? Christians added this part of the prayer as they started meeting together in the early church. Since it wasn't written until later in church life, it isn't included in most Bibles. (Sometimes you'll find it in the footnotes.) But, most of the time, we still use it when we pray the Lord's Prayer.

Think of this part of the prayer as kind of a recap of everything the Lord's Prayer has covered. God's *kingdom* is here and happening. God's *power* provides, strengthens, and forgives. God's love is worthy of praise and *glory*.

Finally, *Amen* is a word used to show agreement that something is true. It's a way to show we believe in everything that's been said. We're ready to see it happen and make it happen. Think of it as shouting out, "Let's go!" or "Let's do this!" at the end of a prayer.

So . . . Let's do this! Wrap up this book with one final quiet time with God. By the way, did you notice you've been praying as you went through this book? Yep. Remember all those quiet times you spent with God writing or drawing something as you thought about the Lord's Prayer? Those. Were. Prayers. Plot twist! Surprise ending!

Prayer is time spent talking with God, so we can pray by speaking, thinking, writing, listening, and even drawing. Amen!

Spend some quiet time with God thinking about this part of the prayer. Here are a few options to inspire your time with God:

A. Now that you've explored the Lord's Prayer, draw a picture of yourself shouting "Amen!"

B. Write as many words you can think of to describe prayer.

C. Write about something you've discovered about God that makes you want to shout, "Amen!"

THE LORD'S PRAYER

Our Father in heaven,
hallowed be your name,
your kingdom come,
your will be done,
on earth as it is in heaven.
Give us today our daily bread.
And forgive us our debts,
as we also have forgiven our debtors.
And lead us not into temptation,
but deliver us from the evil one.
For yours is the kingdom and the power
and the glory forever.

Amen.